YOUR KNOWLEDGE HA

- We will publish your bachelor's and master's thesis, essays and papers

- Your own eBook and book - sold worldwide in all relevant shops

- Earn money with each sale

Upload your text at www.GRIN.com
and publish for free

Bibliographic information published by the German National Library:

The German National Library lists this publication in the National Bibliography; detailed bibliographic data are available on the Internet at http://dnb.dnb.de .

Imprint:

Copyright © 2016 GRIN Verlag, Open Publishing GmbH
Print and binding: Books on Demand GmbH, Norderstedt Germany
ISBN: 9783668336575

This book at GRIN:

http://www.grin.com/en/e-book/342221/the-mobile-navigation-app-osmand-adaptation-for-the-development-of-a

Malte Eilbracht

The Mobile Navigation App 'OsmAnd'. Adaptation for the Development of a Farming Tool for the Agricultural Sector in Thailand

GRIN Publishing

GRIN - Your knowledge has value

Since its foundation in 1998, GRIN has specialized in publishing academic texts by students, college teachers and other academics as e-book and printed book. The website www.grin.com is an ideal platform for presenting term papers, final papers, scientific essays, dissertations and specialist books.

Visit us on the internet:

http://www.grin.com/

http://www.facebook.com/grincom

http://www.twitter.com/grin_com

University of Bristol

Faculty of Social Sciences and Law

School of Economics, Finance and Management

ADAPTION OF THE MOBILE NAVIGATION APP 'OSMAND', IN ORDER
TO DEVELOP A FARMING TOOL FOR THE AGRICULTURAL SECTOR
IN THAILAND

Words: 2186

Table of Contents

List of Tables

Table 1: Important application features of OsmAnd

Table 2: SWOT-analysis of OsmAnd

Table 3: PEST-analysis of 11th National Economic and Social Development Plan of Thailand

Table 4: Detailed Farm Data

Table 5: Possible risks carried by OsmAndFarm and their solution approaches

List of Graphics

Graphic 1: Flow chart of OsmAnd's business process

Graphic 2: Flow chart of OsmAndFarm's business process

Executive Summary

The first part of the essay introduce the map application OsmAnd. The main business processes will be outlined using a flow diagram before illustrating the applications value proposition and revenue model. Finally a SWOT-analysis will identify the applications strength to be the deployment of mobile map data, the customisation of map rendering and the ability of trip recording, audio and video notes and OSM editing.

The second part of the essay uses a PEST-analysis to identify developing potential in a developing country, which was chosen to be Thailand. In consideration of the identified strengths of OsmAnd, the development of the agricultural sector was chosen for further investigation. A short summary of the current situation of the agribusiness follows.

The third part of the essay matches the insights from SWOT- and PEST-analysis to create a new business model. The model is then outlined in a similar manner than initially OsmAnd. Business processes are outlined with the support of a flow diagram, before the changes in value proposition and revenue model are discussed.

The fourth part of the essay sketches potential risks identified during the design process of the new business model and their solution approaches, before concluding that the new model relies on the contribution of the users and the Thai government. Finally it will be recommended, that a good stakeholder management will be needed to overcome the threat caused by this dependencies.

1. Introduction

A Thai proverb says: a tiger relies on his stripes. It's the stripes, which makes a tiger, a tiger and allows him to be competitive in his environment. This essay will, in an analogous manner identify the 'stripes' of the mobile map application OsmAnd. The analogous 'stripes' are here understood as the applications unique value proposition, which allows it to be competitive in a certain business environment. As it is the tigers fade that his stripes bound him to a certain environment, a mobile application can compete globally. Therefore, this essay will outline and analyse the current business model of OsmAnd, before developing a new model based on prior identified strength, to successfully compete in the new environment.

2. Analysis of OsmAnd

On their website, OsmAnd describes their service as a "Global Mobile Map Viewing and Navigation for Online and Offline OSM Maps" (Osmand.net, 2015). This paragraph will outline the essential applications' features, before closely analysing the applications' business model, its business processes, value proposition and revenue model.

2.1 Introduction of the application and its basic features

OsmAnd is a mobile map application, which uses the open data from the OpenStreetMaps[1] project. The application runs on the two market-dominating operating systems, Android and iOS (Osmand.net, 2015); which in the 4th quarter of 2015, with a combined market share of 98.4 % of the global smartphone market (Statista, 2016 a). Therefore, OsmAnd competes with the features listed in Table 1, in a market of approximately 1.8 billion users (Statista, 2016a, 2016b); utilizing the global reach of an e-business.

---

[1] The project is the collaborative work of approximately two million active users, who continuously generate map data all over the world. Hereinafter OSM

2

Table 1: "Important application features of OsmAnd"

	Feature	Appendix I
Map	Highly detailed map of any region in the world	Graphic 1
	Offline mode, including foot, hiking and bike paths	Graphic 1
	Nautical and ski map	Graphic 2, 3
	Customisable over and underlays	Graphic 1
Tools	Trip recording tool, which uses the phone's GPS to track users movements	Graphic 4
	Audio and video notes, which allows users to connect notes to a specific location	Graphic 5
	OSM editing allows the user to map a specific area and directly contribute it to the OSM project	Graphic 6

Source: own table based on Osmand.net (2015)

2.2 Analysis of the business model

OsmAnd's business model combines the content provider model with elements of a community provider (Laudon & Traver, 2015). Graphic 1 shows a flow chart of the applications' main business processes, which will be used to explain the notion of both business models as well as the process of value creation.

Graphic 1: "Flow chart of OsmAnd's business process"

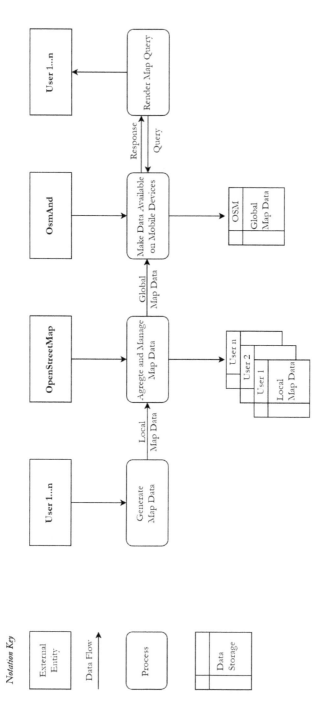

Source: own graphic

4

The graphic illustrates three aspects of OsmAnd's business model. Firstly, as all business processes are transformation steps of map data, it demonstrates how the app is to be a content provider. Secondly, the appearance of the external entity "User 1...n" at both ends of the value creation process, indicates that a sub group of end-users might be identical with cartographers, who initially generated the map data for OpenStreetMap. This gives OsmAnd an element as a community provider. Thirdly, the graphic indicates clearly the subsequent position of OsmAnd in the value creation process; their focus is set on the supply of mobile map data, rather than the data generation, data aggregation or data management.

After outlining the general business model and its main processes the following paragraph will analyse, how the created value is proposed to consumers and how it is transformed into revenue.

Kambil, Ginsberg and Bloch (1998) define 'Value Proposition' as the degree to which a product or service satisfies consumers' needs. In the widest sense, OsmAnd satisfies the need for geographical information. As this need is attempted to be satisfied by all products in the market, the added value of OsmAnd has to be identified. Kambil (1997) and Bakos (1998), suggest personalisation and customisation, amongst other things, to be successful e-commerce value propositions (Laudon & Traver, 2015). The in Table 1 listed application features indicate that OsmAnd has positioned themselves with a mass customisation strategy in the market, while the value creation takes places in, what Doligalski (2015) calls a 'Do-it-yourself-customisation'. OsmAnd is a non-diversified mass product, delivering identical value propositions to all users, which can then be adjusted to personal needs to finally create a customised product (Doligalski, 2015). The high degree of customisability of the rendering process, appears to be the unique value proposition of the application.

After identifying the applications value proposition, the applied revenue model has to be evaluated. Google Play as well as Apple's App Store offer the download of the application for free (Play.google.com, 2016; App Store, 2016). The application comes with full online service, customisable settings and ten regional offline maps. Further offline data, the nautical map as well as the information of counter lines are optional in-app purchases (Play.google.com, 2016; App Store, 2016). The use of in-app purchases to generate revenue corresponds with, what Liu, Au and Choi (2014, p.2) referring to (Hayes, 2008) describe as freemium; "a business model by which a service or a product is offered free of charge, but a premium is charged for advanced features, functionality, or related products and services".

Table 2 aggregates above-noted results in the form of a SWOT-analysis (Awais, 2012).

Table 2: "SWOT-analysis of OsmAnd"

Strength	Weakness
Deployment of mobile map data	Reliance on OSM map data
Customisation of map rendering	Reliance on user contribution
Trip recording	
Audio and video notes	
OSM editing	
Opportunity	**Threat**
Offline mode	Competitors (Google maps, Bing maps, Here map, MapQuest)
	Availability of mobile internet connection

Source: own table

3. Identification of possible contribution to the e-commerce in a developing country

This paragraph attempts to identify possible contributions of OsmAnd, to the e-commerce of a developing country. For this purpose it is referred to Laudon and Traver's (2015, p.49) notion on e-commerce, as "the use of the internet, […] and mobile apps to transact business", where a transaction "involves the exchange of value […] in return for products and services".

To draw a more specific case, this essay will refer to Thailand as a developing economy. The Worldbank classifies Thailand, with a GNI per capita of 5,780$, to be a middle-income economy (Data.worldbank.org, 2016). As "[l]ow- and middle-income economies are sometimes referred to as developing economies" (Data.worldbank.org, 2013), Thailand can be identified as a developing country.

To identify possible contributions, a PEST analysis (Shabanova et al., 2015) was carried out to identify developing potential in the country; the results were subsequently matched with the strengths of OsmAnd, which where prior identified in a SWOT analysis.

For a more efficient identification of developing potential, the scope of the PEST analysis was narrowed down to 'The Eleventh National Economic and Social Development Plan'.

The results are displayed in Table 3.

Table 3: "PEST-analysis of the Eleventh National Economic and Social Development Plan of Thailand"

Political	Economic
"Thai people are now more active in politics and ready to express opinions. However, political conflicts and the unrest in the southernmost provinces have continued. These have affected the economy, daily life, confidence in Thailand by other countries and peace in Thai society" (p. v)	"Thai economy has experienced moderate growth with stability. While the industrial sector has played a major role in production, the agricultural sector remains a key source of income" (p. iv)
"Public administration is ineffective" (p. v)	"The economic structure is too unstable to assure sustainable development" (p. vi)
"National security remains critical" (p. vii)	"Strengthening of the agricultural sector and security of food and energy" (p. xiv)
"Corruption remains a critical problem" (p.14)	"Strengthen water and land management to support food security and economic restructuring" (p.19)
Social	**Technological**
"Although potential development opportunities are provided for all Thai people, educational quality, child intelligence, risk behaviors for health, and low labor productivity have remained major concerns" (p. v)	"Thailand must base its future development on knowledge, technology and innovation" (p. vii)
"The demographic structure has changed as the older population increases, and those younger and of working age decrease" (p. vi)	
"Social values and traditions have deteriorated" (p. vi) "Thai society maintains high values and culture" (p. vii)	

Source: own table based on The Eleventh National Economic and Social Development Plan 2012-2016, (2011)

The SWOT-analysis identified the deployment of mobile map data, the customisation of map rendering, the ability of trip recording, audio and video notes and OSM editing, to be strength of

OsmAnd. These technological capabilities regarding the management of geographical information could be utilized to strengthen the agricultural sector of the Thai economy, a development goal, identified by the PEST-analysis. The linkage between the capabilities of OsmAnd and the development of Thai agribusiness could be 'the usage of land'.

To develop further insights in the current situation of the Thai agricultural sector, the conceptions of the Eleventh National Economic and Social Development Plan 2012-2016, (2011, pp. 58-61) were summarised as follows:

The agricultural sector accounts to 8.3% of the GDP and provides income for approximately 6.9 million households. In recent years the agribusiness was weakened, on the basis of low production and unsustainable framing. Major divers for the low productivity were the high share of farmers living under the poverty line and the farmer decline of 1.9% p.a. Unsustainable farming methods recorded by the government were the exploitation of natural resources without consideration of restoration as well as the use chemical fertilizers and pesticides. Drought, infertile land, water shortage and an inadequate infrastructure lead to further deterioration.

On the basis of the above-noted analysis was a business model developed, which will help the development of the agricultural sector, by gathering farm specific information, enriching them with an up-to-date market data and information about sustainable framing, to deliver customized farming plans to every user. The following paragraph will outline the business model in more detail.

4. Discussion of the new business model

First and foremost, Graphic 2 will be used to provide a summary of the new business model[2] and its process of value creation. It follows a discussion on essential modifications of the value proposition and the revenue model, before potential risks and challenges will be identified.

---

[2] Conceptually named "OsmAndFarm"

Graphic 2: "Flow chart of OsmAndFarm's business process"

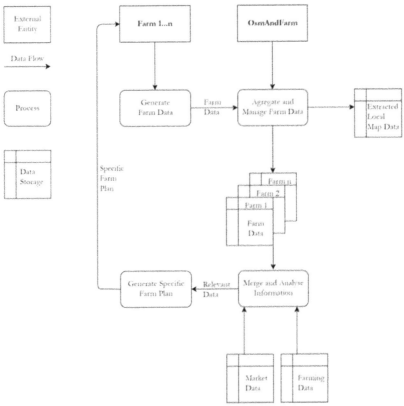

Source: own graphic

During the installation of the application on the framer's device, an account has to be created. The purpose of an account is to link the gathered information to a specific farm and to later deliver the customised farming plan to the correct user. After this set-up, the farmer can begin using the track recording tool and the OSM editing plugin to map out his fields and add the information of which crop he is culturing on each field.

While the mapping of the field remains a one-time process, crop information need to be updated with the crop rotation. The aggregated farm data, as listed in Table 3, will automatically be transferred to OsmAndFarm[3].

Table 4: "Detailed Farm Data"

Information
Location of the farm
Number of fields
Size of each field
Crop on each field
Location of each field

Source: own table

Subsequently, these information are merged with relevant market and farming data. Market information could include current market prices of seeds, fertilizer or other input variables as well as the current and forecasted prices, supply and demand of crops. Relevant framing data could consist of sustainable farming methods, fertility of local soil, weather, the availability of water or ideal crop rotations. After the merger, the entirety of all available information are analysed to develop a customised farming plan for the user.

This new business model does not only affect the business process and value creation, but it also has a significant impact on the value proposition and the revenue model.

Recalling the definition of 'Value Proposition' by Kambil, Ginsberg and Bloch (1998), as the degree to which a product or service satisfies consumers' needs; three parameters need to be evaluated. Firstly, it has to be reviewed whether the product or service has changed. Secondly, it has to

---

[3] Extracted, relevant map data will also transferred to OsmAnd to contribute to the old business model.
See APPENDIX II

be reviewed whether there was a shift in the consumer base and, thirdly, it has to be verified that the service still fulfils the consumers' needs. As the service of the new business model has drastically changed, from the supply of mobile geographical information with a high degree of customisability, to the supply of customised farming plans, it is expected that the consumer base likewise, has shifted towards Thai farmers.

Still, there is a simultaneously value creation for another stakeholder, the Thai government (Frow & Payne, 2011), as it can be argued, that the service of OsmAndFarm is also the development of the Thai agribusiness, which is a documented goal of the Thai government (The Eleventh National Economic and Social Development Plan, 2011). Applying this perspective, the Thai government becomes the consumer of the service.

This example illustrates that different "stakeholder may have different value propositions" (Murtaza, Ikram & Basit, 2010, p.557) towards the same product or service. However, the distinct value propositions of the Thai farmers and the Thai government are per se negligible, as they occur simultaneously. By providing customised farming plans to Thai agriculturalist, the value of a developed agricultural sector will be co-created for the Thai government.

However, the different value propositions become essentials for the design of the revenue model. Laudon and Traver's (2015, p.49) notion on e-commerce, as "the use of the internet, […] and mobile apps to transact business", where a transaction "involves the exchange of value […] in return for products and services" provide guidance to set up a new revenue model. As the service remains the same, regardless which stakeholder will be addressed it has to be evaluated which party will exchange the grater value for the service.

As the majority of Thai farmers live under the poverty-line, (The Eleventh National Economic and Social Development Plan, 2011) and are already providing their work of mapping fields and the data input, it appears reasonable to focus on the Thai government for the construction of a new revenue model.

Laudon and Traver (2015) suggest a sales revenue model. Every time a customised farming plan is sent to an agriculturalist, the Thai government will be charged a certain fee, as this service simultaneously creates the value of a slightly developed agricultural sector. The sales model moreover appears to be fair, as the revenue of the company is directly linked to the value creation for the government.

5. Outline of identified possible risks

Prior to the final conclusion, the author wishes to outline some of the identified risks of the new business model "OsmAndFarm".

The key issue of the new model, is the interaction with the Thai farmers. Initially, it has to be evaluated how farmers can be addressed, as their contribution is necessary for the value creation. Table 5 lists the identified key risks, describes the problem and possible solution approaches.

Table 5: "Possible risks carried by OsmAndFarm and their solution approaches"

Key risks	Description of the problem	Solution approaches
Addressing the farmer	Contacting and addressing the approximately 6.9 million farming households in Thailand, most commonly living in rural areas	Support of the Thai Government
Missing technology	Some farmers might not own a mobile device, with the necessary technological standard	Subsidy of smartphones for participating farmers by the Thai government
Cognitive barrier	Farmers might have cognitive barriers to e-commerce, as described by Ksherti (2007), that is, a lack of understanding of the benefits, a lack of trust in the technology and/or a lack of general computer skills	Simple user interface in the Thai language and highly automated processes, requiring a minimum of human input
Reliance on contribution	Farmers might not be willing to contribute or not regularly update the necessary information	Highlighting the value proposition for farmers and their personal benefits of participation
Acceptance of recommendations	Farmers might not be willing to accept the recommendations of the farming plan, which would decrease the degree of agricultural development	Highlighting the value proposition for farmers and their personal benefits of participation

Source: own table

6. Conclusion

The analysis of the business model of OsmAnd identified the strength of the application to be, the deployment of mobile map data, the customisation of map rendering and the ability of trip recording, audio and video notes and OSM editing. A subsequent PEST analysis of the Thai economy found various development goals, where the development of the agricultural sector showed the greatest potential to match the strengths of OsmAnd. Based on the acquired insights, a new business model was developed, which builds on OsmAnd's capabilities in the management and deployment of geographical data to generate and supply customised farming plans to participating agriculturalists. During the discussion of the changes in the value proposition revenue model and possible risks, it was found that the new model OsmAndFarm relies on the contribution and participation of the farmers, as well as the support of the Thai government. Nevertheless, stakeholder management could overcome this dependence by highlighting that the largest part of the value creation for all parties is done by OsmAndFarm.

Bibliography

App Store. (2016). *OsmAnd Maps on the App Store*. [online] Available at: https://itunes.apple.com/app/apple-store/id934850257?mt=8 [Accessed 26 Apr. 2016].

Awais, M. (2012). Advanced SWOT Analysis of E-Commerce. *International Journal of Computer Science Issues*, 9(2), pp. 569-574

Bakos, Y. (1998). The emerging role of electronic marketplaces on the Internet. *Communications of the ACM*, 41(8), pp.35-42.

Data.worldbank.org. (2013). *New Country Classifications | Data*. [online] Available at: http://data.worldbank.org/news/new-country-classifications [Accessed 26 Apr. 2016].

Data.worldbank.org. (2016). *Thailand | Data*. [online] Available at: http://data.worldbank.org/country/thailand [Accessed 26 Apr. 2016].

Doligalski, T. (2015). *Internet-based customer value management*. Heidelberg: Springer.

Frow, P. and Payne, A. (2011). A stakeholder perspective of the value proposition concept. *European Journal of Marketing*, 45(1/2), pp.223-240.

Hayes, T. (2008). *Jump point: How Network Culture Is Revolutionizing Business*. New York: McGraw-Hill.

Kambil, A. (1997). Doing business in the wired world. *Computer*, 30(5), pp.56-61.

Kambil, A., Ginsberg, A., Bloch, M. (1998). *Reinventing Value Proposition*. Working Paper: NYU Center for Research on Information Systems.

Kshetri, N. (2007). Barriers to e-commerce and competitive business models in developing countries: A case study. *Electronic Commerce Research and Applications*, 6(4), pp.443-452.

Laudon, K. and Traver, C. (2015). E-Commerce 2015. 11th ed. Boston, Columbus, Indianapolis: Pearson Education Limited.

Liu, C., Au, Y. and Choi, H. (2014). Effects of Freemium Strategy in the Mobile App Market: An Empirical Study of Google Play. *Journal of Management Information Systems*, 31(3), pp.326-354.

Murtaza, G., Ikram, N., Basit A. (2010). A Framework for Eliciting Value Proposition from Stakeholders. *WSEAS TRANSACTIONS on COMPUTERS*, 9(6), pp.557-572

Osmand.net. (2015). *OsmAnd - Offline Mobile Maps and Navigation*. [online] Available at: http://osmand.net/ [Accessed 24 Apr. 2016]

Play.google.com. (2016). [online] Available at: https://play.google.com/store/apps/details?id=net.osmand [Accessed 26 Apr. 2016].

Shabanova, L.B.; Akhmadeev, G.N.; Ismagilova, L.N.; Salimov, M.G. (2015). PEST - Analysis and SWOT - Analysis as the most important tools to strengthen the competitive advantages of commercial enterprises. *Mediterranean Journal of Social Sciences*, 6(3), pp.705-709

Statista. (2016a). *Smartphone OS global market share 2009-2015 | Statistic*. [online] Available at: http://www.statista.com/statistics/266136/global-market-share-held-by-smartphone-operating-systems/ [Accessed 26 Apr. 2016].

Statista. (2016b). *Smartphone users worldwide 2014-2019 | Statistic*. [online] Available at: http://www.statista.com/statistics/330695/number-of-smartphone-users-worldwide/ [Accessed 26 Apr. 2016].

The Eleventh National Economic and Social Development Plan (2012-2016). (2011). Bangkok: National Economic and Social Development Board Office of the Prime Minister.

APPENDIX I

Source of Graphic 1 – 6: Osmand.net. (2015).

Graphic 1: "Highly detailed map including foot and bike path with satellite underlay"

Graphic 2: "Nautical map"

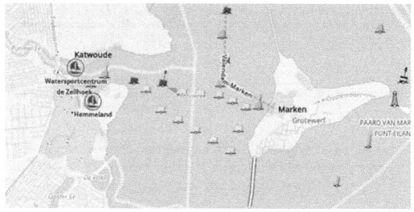

Graphic 3: "Ski Map of St. Anton"

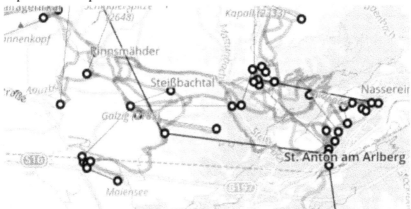

Graphic 4: "Trip recording in Dresden"

Graphic 5: "Audio and video notes in Vienna"

Graphic 6: "OpenStreetMap editing in Copenhagen"

APPENDIX II

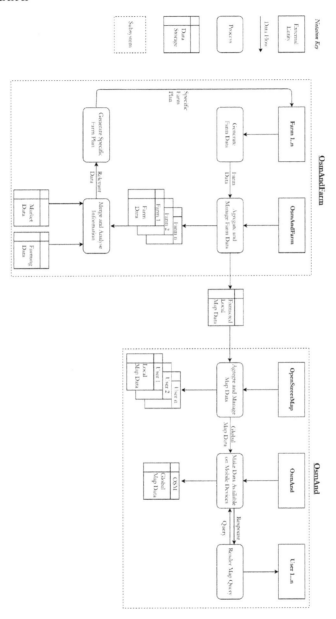

YOUR KNOWLEDGE HAS VALUE

- We will publish your bachelor's and master's thesis, essays and papers

- Your own eBook and book - sold worldwide in all relevant shops

- Earn money with each sale

Upload your text at www.GRIN.com and publish for free